I0407934

Eagle
Coloring Book
For Adults

30 Hand Drawn, Doodle and Folk Art Paisley, Henna and Zentangle Style Eagle Coloring Pages

By
Louise Ford

Copyright © 2017
All rights Reserved.

ISBN-13: 978-1543166279
ISBN-10: 154316627X

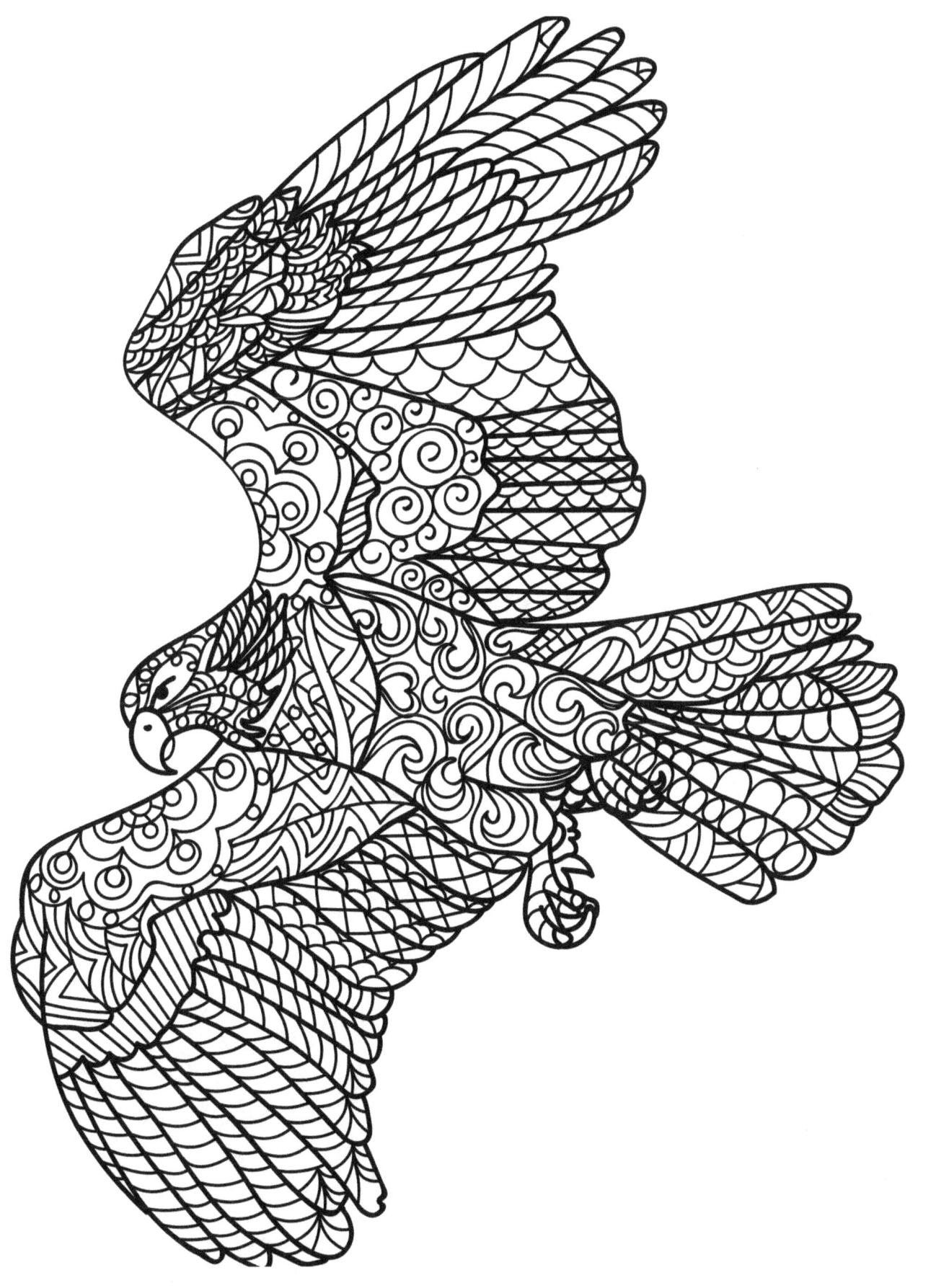

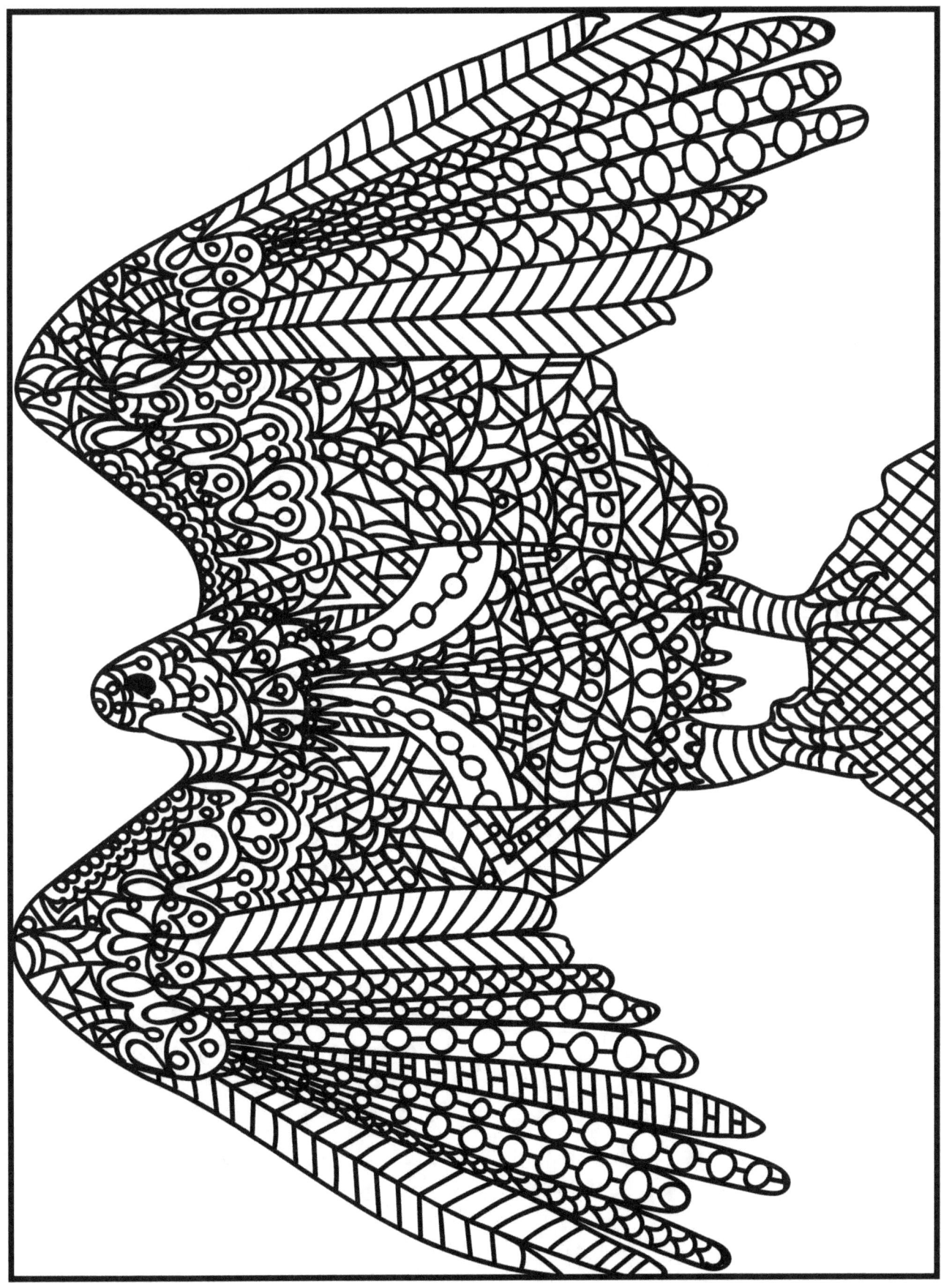

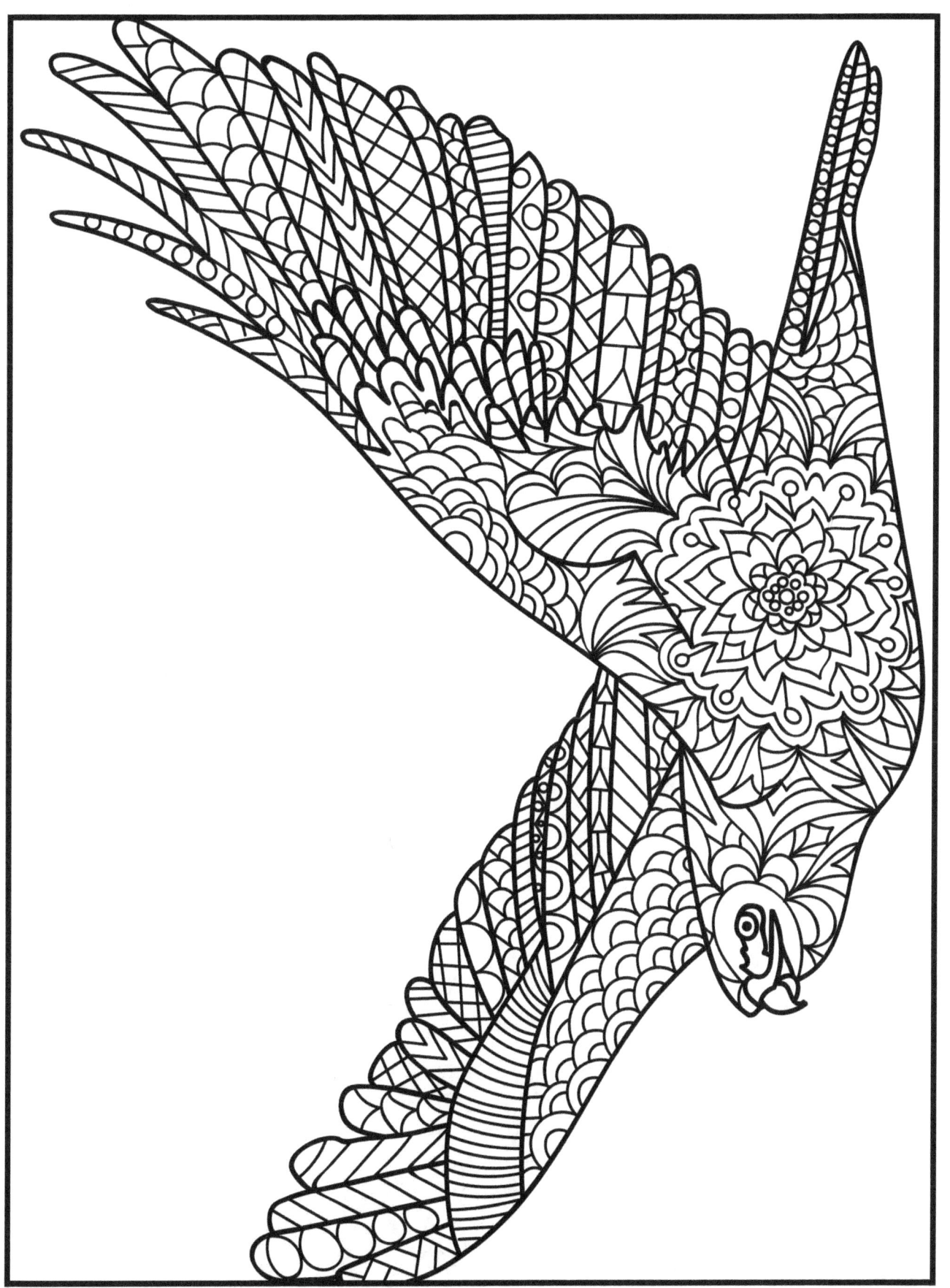

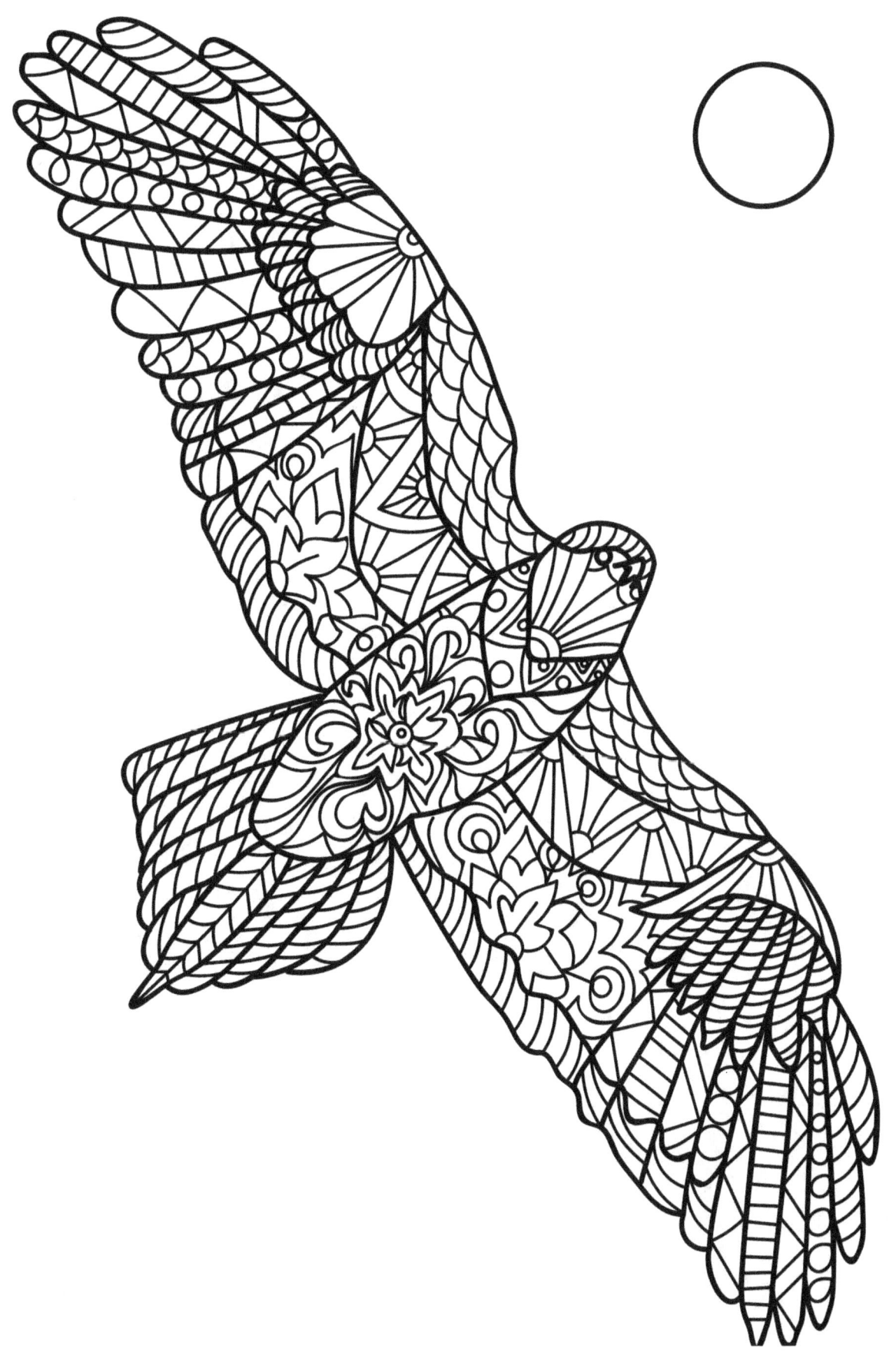

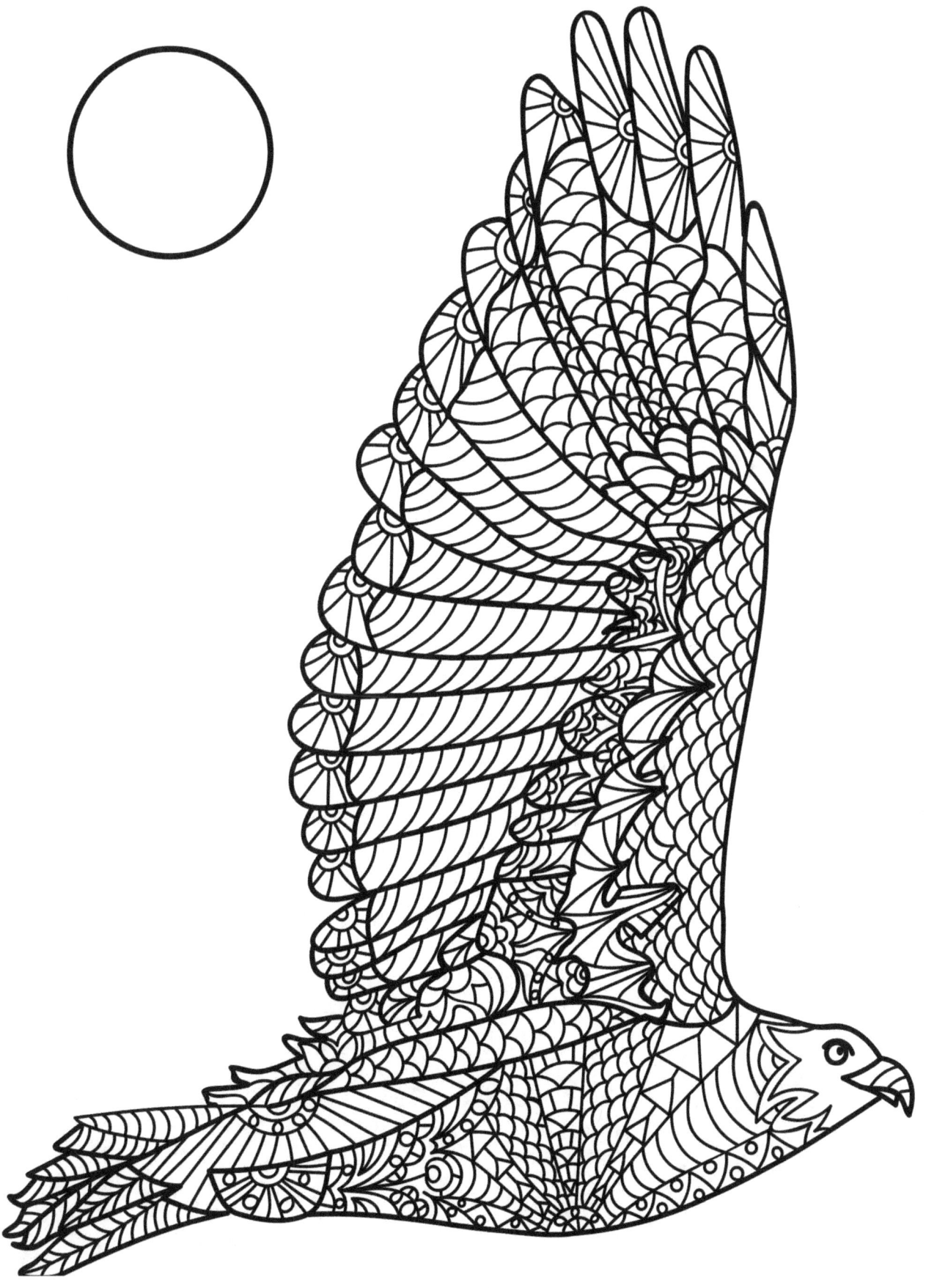

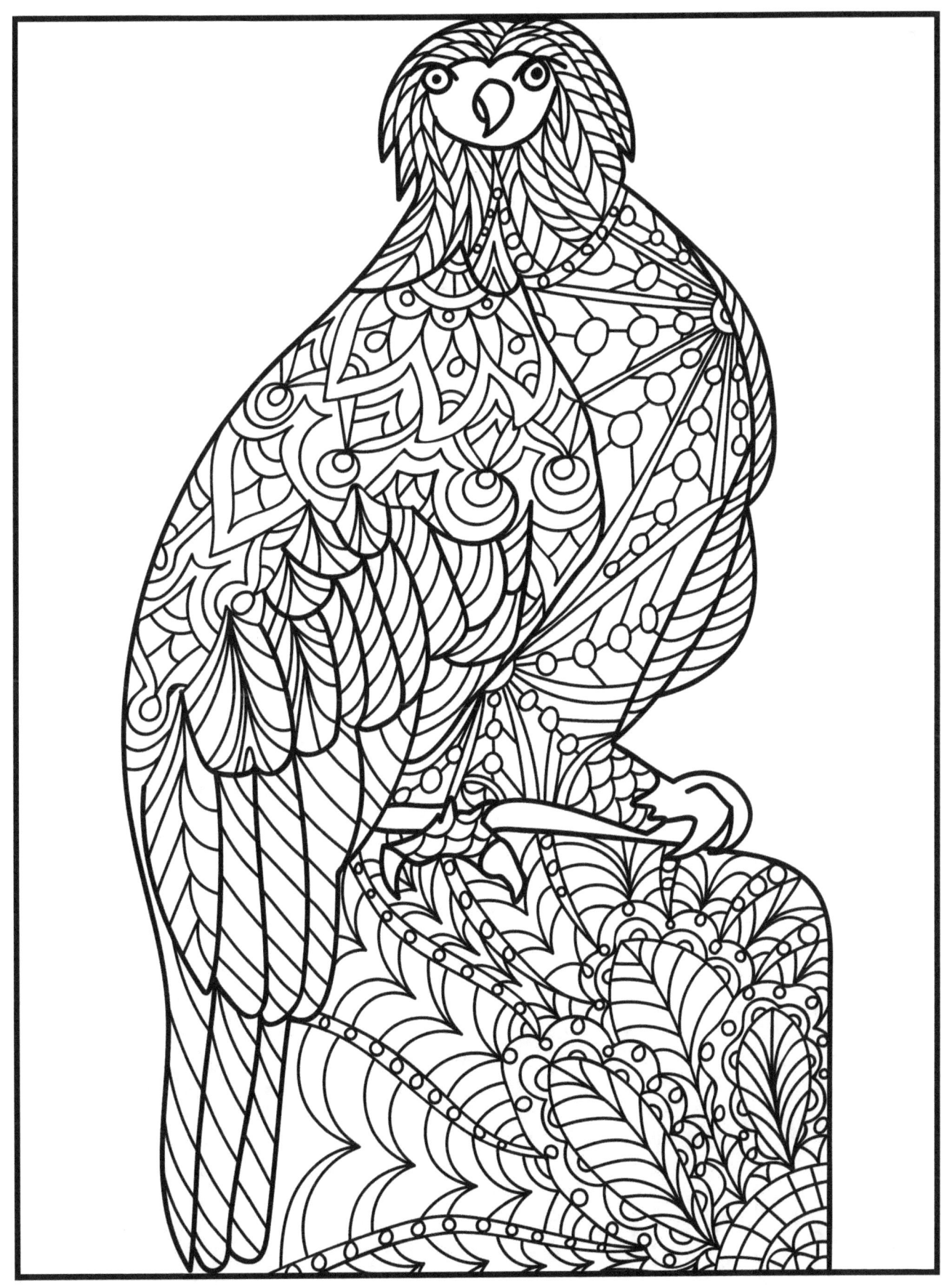

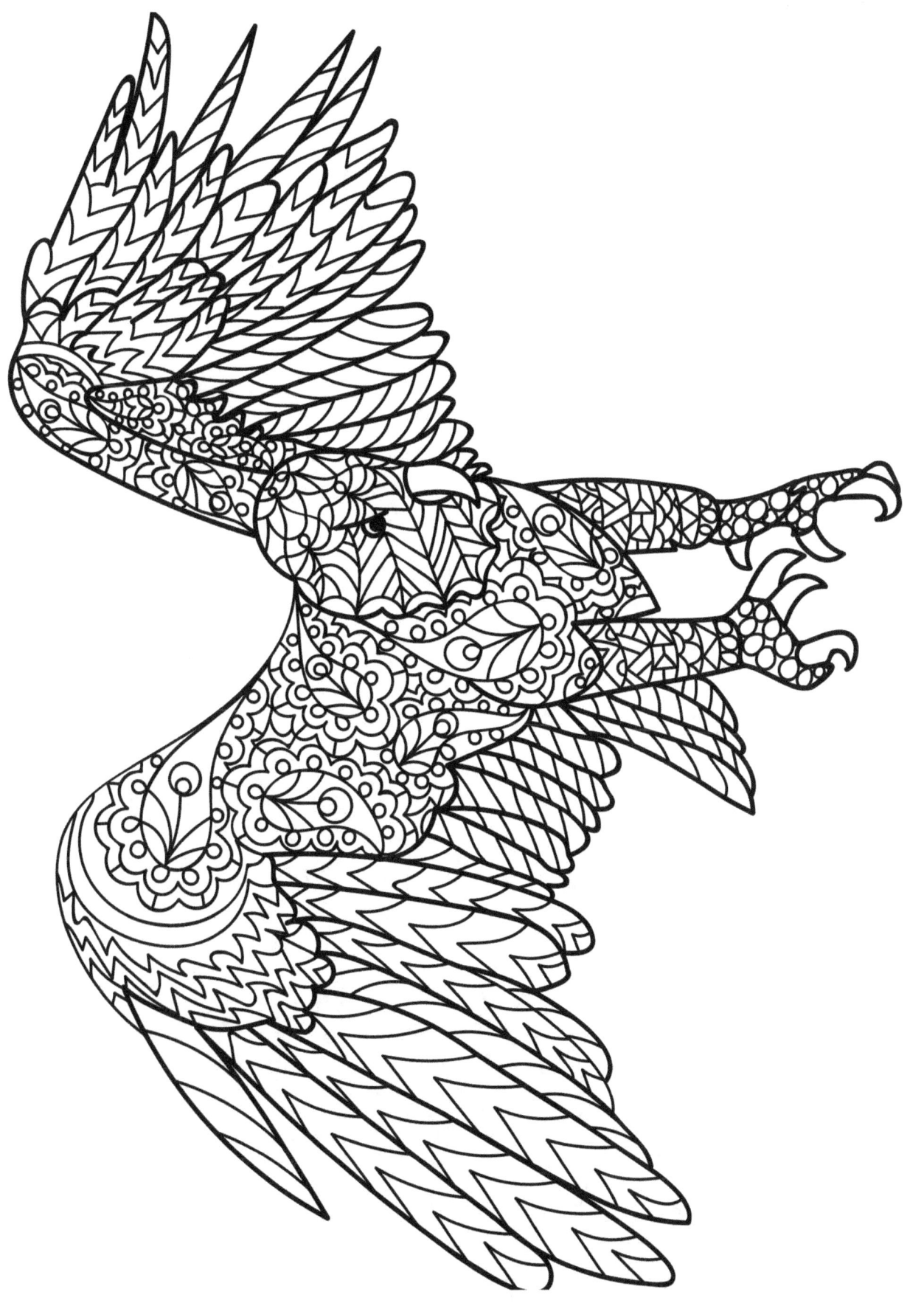

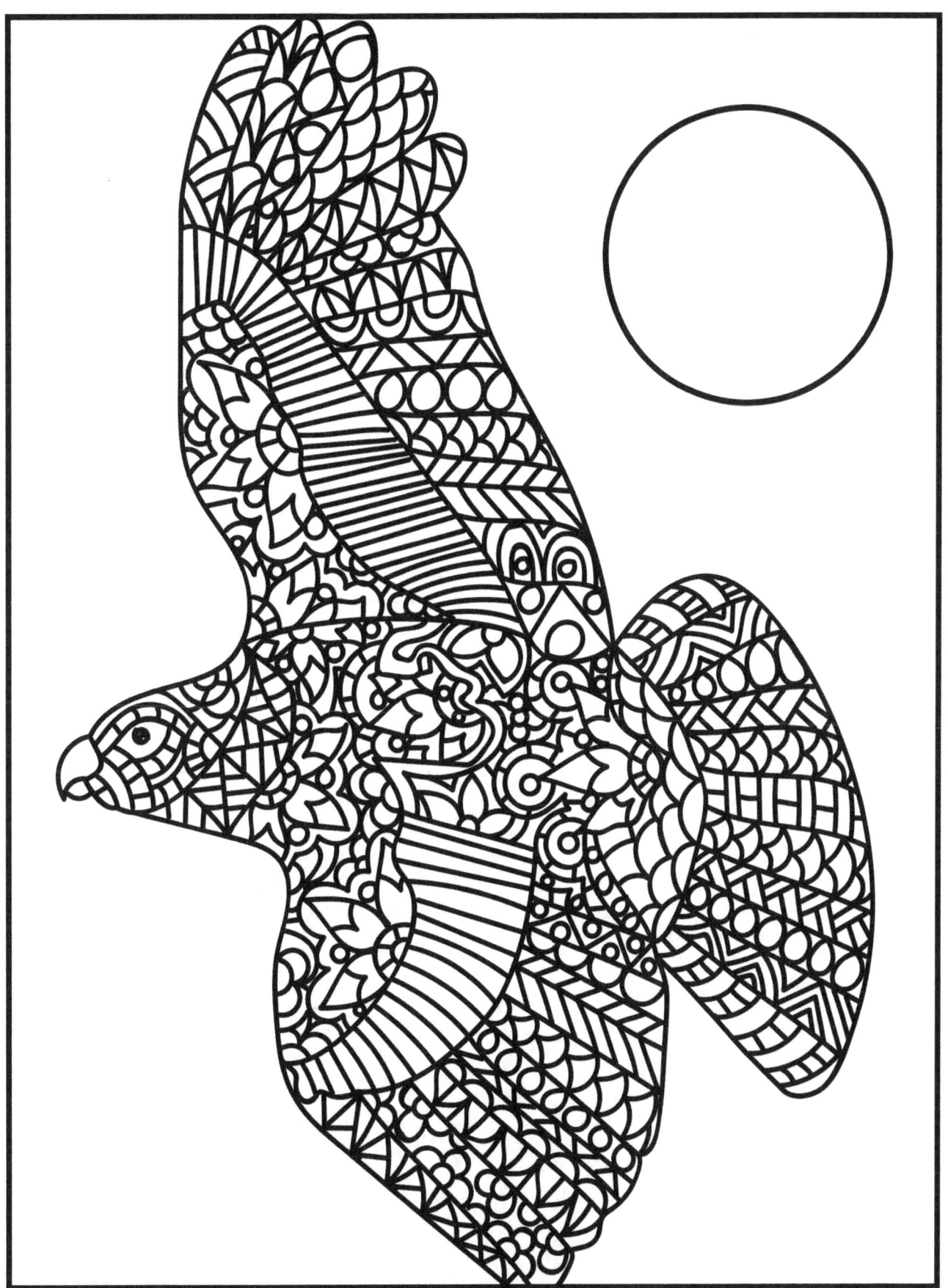

www.ingramcontent.com/pod-product-compliance
Lightning Source LLC
Chambersburg PA
CBHW081418280526
45788CB00009B/3152